3.95

WITHDRAWN

THE STORY OF THE
ORANGE
BOWL

by Dave Campbell

abdopublishing.com

Published by Abdo Publishing, a division of ABDO, PO Box 398166, Minneapolis, Minnesota 55439. Copyright © 2016 by Abdo Consulting Group, Inc. International copyrights reserved in all countries. No part of this book may be reproduced in any form without written permission from the publisher. SportsZone™ is a trademark and logo of Abdo Publishing.

Printed in the United States of America, North Mankato, Minnesota
052015
092015

Cover Photo: Lynne Sladky/AP Images, cover
Interior Photos: Lynne Sladky/AP Images, 1, 28, 38, 39; Alan Diaz/AP Images, 4; AP Images, 7, 8, 16, 18, 22, 42, 43; John Raoux/AP Images, 10; Orange Bowl/Collegiate Images/Getty Images, 12, 15; Jim Bourdier/AP Images, 21; Mark Elias/AP Images, 24; Ray Fairall/AP Images, 27; Hans Deryk/AP Images, 30; Susan Walsh/AP Images, 33, 35; Joe Cavareta/AP Images, 34; J. Pat Carter/AP Images, 36, 40

Editor: Patrick Donnelly
Series Designer: Nikki Farinella

Library of Congress Control Number: 2015931693

Cataloging-in-Publication Data
Campbell, Dave.
 The story of the Orange Bowl / Dave Campbell.
   p. cm. -- (Bowl games of college football)
Includes bibliographical references and index.
ISBN 978-1-62403-889-1
1. Orange Bowl (Football game)--History--Juvenile literature. 2. Football--United States--Juvenile literature. 3. College sports--Juvenile literature. I. Title.
796.332--dc23

                                        2015931693

TABLE OF CONTENTS

The annual Orange Bowl parade was a big part of the pageantry surrounding the game throughout its first 60 years.

ORANGE BOWL HISTORY:
BIG DREAMS
TO BIG TIME

Hurricanes and Huskers. Seminoles and Sooners. Some of the biggest games and biggest names in college football history have helped make the Orange Bowl one of the most celebrated events in sports.

The game dates to the mid-1930s. Like many US cities at the time, Miami, Florida, was struggling through the Great Depression. Local businessmen were trying to attract tourists and boost the economy. The Rose Bowl in California stood alone on the college football stage. But if California could have a bowl game, people in Miami figured Florida could, too. It already had sunshine, beaches, and palm trees. Throw in a New Year's Day game as the featured attraction?

That would sound pretty good to northerners considering a winter vacation.

Miami was once a quiet fishing village on the Atlantic coast of Florida. Today it is a fast-moving, glamorous metropolis. Like the city itself, the Orange Bowl grew from a modest beginning. It owes much of its success to a tireless promoter named Earnie Seiler.

The Palm Festival was the original name of this game. Seiler once stood on the street encouraging people to come in for free to fill the bleachers. After that two-year warm-up, the first Orange Bowl was played on January 1, 1935, when Bucknell beat the University of Miami. The Bison were so concerned about the tropical heat they brought 280 gallons (1,060 L) of their own water from Pennsylvania to stay hydrated. The water may have helped, because Bucknell won 26–0.

The 1939 game truly made the Orange Bowl a big-time event, thanks to Seiler's persuasion. He wanted the mighty Oklahoma Sooners to play in that year's game. So he traveled to Oklahoma to make his case, plastering posters and sidewalk-chalk messages around campus. The Sooners were impressed. They took less money than other bowls were offering and agreed to come to Miami to play against the Tennessee Volunteers.

Billy Jefferson of Mississippi State plunges through a crowd of Georgetown defenders to score a touchdown in the 1941 Orange Bowl.

By the mid-1950s, the game was broadcast on national television. The pregame parade was shown on TV too. The floats got brighter. The hype grew louder. The party got bigger. Seiler even brought in fans to spread the scent of orange blossom perfume from the top of the stadium. The fancier, the better, he believed.

The Orange Bowl eventually signed a contract with the Big 8 Conference to give its champion, often Nebraska or Oklahoma, an automatic invitation to Miami.

That Nebraska–Oklahoma rivalry grew into one of the most intense in the country. It was so intriguing that

Aerial view of the Orange Bowl before the 1938 game between Auburn and Michigan State

the Orange Bowl even staged a rematch one year. The Huskers beat the Sooners in the 1978 regular season, but they lost to Missouri and ended the season tied with Oklahoma for first place in the conference. When the two teams met again in Miami, the Sooners won 31–24.

By this point the Orange Bowl was a prime destination. Nebraska fans even started a tradition of tossing oranges onto the field at games late in the season, looking forward to another journey to Miami.

Oklahoma and Nebraska have played in the Orange Bowl the most of any teams by far. Through 2014, the Sooners had made 18 appearances, the Huskers 17. Many times, the national championship was determined at the Orange Bowl stadium, just west of downtown Miami.

Some of those trips were devastating for Nebraska and its dedicated fans. The 1983 team was ranked number one all season. The Huskers dominated almost every team they played. They even scored 84 points in a September win at Minnesota. But their opponent in the fiftieth Orange Bowl was Miami, and the Hurricanes were on their home field.

Miami built a 17-0 lead behind two touchdown passes from freshman quarterback Bernie Kosar, a future NFL standout for the Cleveland Browns. The Huskers rallied from a 31-17 deficit in the fourth quarter, however, and scored a touchdown with 48 seconds left. That put them down by only one point. Huskers coach Tom Osborne called for a two-point conversion. The pass by Turner Gill was incomplete. That handed the Hurricanes their first national title. The teams met in the Orange Bowl three more times in the next 11 years.

Traditions do not always last. The Big 8 expanded to become the Big 12 Conference in 1996. After that,

Nebraska quarterback Turner Gill, *left*, is swallowed up by Miami's Kevin Fagan in the classic 1984 Orange Bowl.

the conference champion was slated instead for the Fiesta Bowl in Arizona. The Orange Bowl had a new tie-in with the Atlantic Coast Conference (ACC). The whole bowl system was in a state of change as the twenty-first century dawned. Fans pushed more than ever for a true national championship.

For many years, polls determined the national champion. From 1998 to 2013, the Orange Bowl was part of the Bowl Championship Series (BCS). The BCS bowls were the most important in college football. Each year one was designated to be the national title game. But polls still determined the two best teams. Fans continued to push for a true national championship. Finally, the College Football Playoff was created for the 2014 season. The four-team tournament is designed to crown an undisputed champion. The Orange Bowl was picked as one of the six bowls to be a part of it. It will host a national semifinal game once every three years.

No matter the format, the Orange Bowl has continued to be a major event and a big business. The game on January 3, 2014, was a thriller. Clemson beat Ohio State 40–35. For qualifying, each school earned $17 million. Attendance at Sun Life Stadium was 72,080. An estimated 11.4 million people watched on TV. Earnie Seiler would have been proud.

EVERYONE LOVES A PARADE

The King Orange Jamboree parade was a popular event. In many years requests to participate would come from more than 200 marching bands around the country. The first New Year's Eve version was in 1935. Floats were lit as the procession went down Biscayne Boulevard. By 1954, the parade was televised. The event lasted until 2002, when bowl officials decided to end the tradition because it was losing money.

The 1939 Orange Bowl featured two of the strongest teams in the country, Tennessee and Oklahoma.

2

1939
SEILER THE
SALESMAN
Tennessee vs. Oklahoma

The 1939 game made the Orange Bowl a big-time event. Earnie Seiler, the recreation director for the city of Miami, was determined to bring one of the powerhouse programs to his place. So he traveled west to Norman, Oklahoma, to persuade the Sooners to play in the Orange Bowl.

Representatives from the Sugar and Cotton Bowls were offering more money, but Seiler was not discouraged. He covered the campus with posters featuring Miami's breathtaking scenery. He even helped write "On to Miami" in chalk on the sidewalks. His personal sales pitch put the Orange Bowl over the top. Oklahoma was on board.

Sooners coach Tom Stidham called Bob Neyland, his friend and fellow coach at the University Tennessee, and the Volunteers were in, too. Suddenly, Miami was the spot for biggest game of that 1938 season, matching two undefeated teams. The Orange Bowl stadium was supposed to hold only 22,000 people at that point. More than 32,000 showed up for this one.

These Sooners were the first in the program's rich history to achieve a national ranking. Their defense was dominant. It allowed only 12 points total while the Sooners won all 10 of their regular-season games.

But Tennessee was just as tough. The Volunteers were the Southeast Conference (SEC) champions. They allowed a total of only 16 points in their 10–0 regular season. The next year, Tennessee would not give up a single point the entire regular season. The seeds of that stinginess were planted against Oklahoma on New Year's Day 1939.

Tennessee's coach was more formally known as General Robert Reese Neyland. He was a former army officer who led his team as though he were still in the military. Tennessee's stadium is named after him today. Neyland demanded discipline and attention to detail from his players. His single-wing offense was a popular system of that time. It featured four players

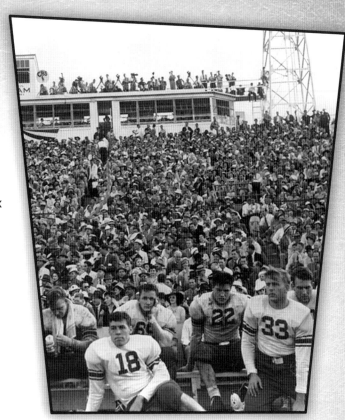

Oklahoma players look glum as they absorb a 17–0 beating against Tennessee in the 1939 Orange Bowl.

in the backfield who all ran the ball well. They rarely passed the ball. A tailback named George "Bad News" Cafego led the Volunteers. He was a punishing runner who helped Tennessee set the tone for a rough game that became known as "The Orange Brawl." On the first play, Cafego knocked over an Oklahoma player with a devastating block.

"He had to be taken out of the game. I don't think Oklahoma got over it," Cafego said.

Tennessee used an aggressive blocking style that Oklahoma was not used to. The Sooners thought it should be illegal. Tennessee took 130 total yards

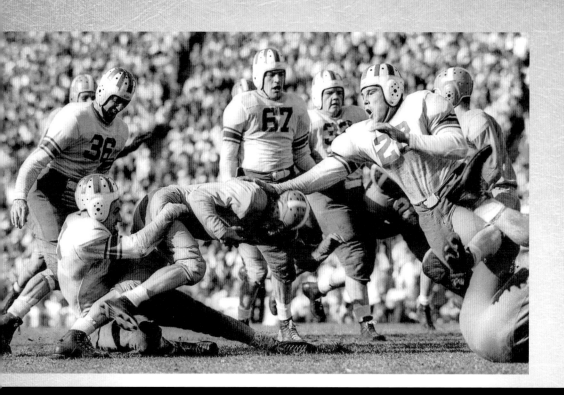

Tennessee's Buist Warren, *center*, is brought down by a horde of Oklahoma defenders during the 1939 Orange Bowl.

in penalties. Oklahoma was flagged for 90 yards. Two players were kicked out of the game, one from each team. The officials had to stop the action often to get the guys to cool off.

Many players were injured and had to leave the game. Even a Volunteers cheerleader was knocked unconscious at one point. She was injured when a Tennessee player accidentally crashed into her as he went out of bounds at the end of a play.

The Sooners were at a disadvantage before the ball was even kicked off, though. Starting running backs

Howard McCarty and Bill Jennings were hurt, and they did not play. The Sooners were the bigger team, but they were slower, too. The Volunteers were confident they could win with their speed and their stamina.

Tennessee had a 10–0 lead at halftime, and the final score was 17–0. All of the statistics pointed toward the Volunteers. They totaled 260 yards, compared with only 94 for the Sooners. Oklahoma lost three fumbles, and Tennessee gave up only one.

Frank Ivy played end for the Sooners. He summarized the frustrating experience with a story of the team's return to Norman.

"There was a big crowd to meet us, and several of us got off the train on the other side of the track and sneaked away," Ivy said. "We had played so poorly that we were ashamed to be seen. It took us a long time to get over it."

STADIUM SWITCH

With money from the US government helping pay for the project, the Orange Bowl stadium opened in time for the game on January 1, 1938. The horseshoe-shaped stadium hosted the Orange Bowl game until December 31, 1996. That year it switched to the home of the National Football League's (NFL's) Miami Dolphins. One more Orange Bowl was played at the original stadium two years later. Then it moved for good. The Dolphins' Sun Life Stadium remains the Orange Bowl's home. It opened in 1987 and holds 75,000 people.

3

1969
PEPPER'S
EXTRA PLAYER
Penn State vs. Kansas

Penn State earned its reputation with a feisty coach named Joe Paterno. His became one of the famous faces of the game. He had thick dark hair and tinted glasses with frames that were just as thick. Paterno won 409 games in his 46 years as head coach at Penn State. This unmatched career started in 1966, and by his third season the Nittany Lions were on their way to the Orange Bowl.

Nebraska and Oklahoma usually controlled the Big 8 Conference, which was around from 1960–1995. But Kansas was crowned champion one time. That was in 1968. Coach Pepper Rodgers's Jayhawks lost to Oklahoma that season but still earned the Orange Bowl bid based on the strength of their other victories.

The Jayhawks had a memorable finish to their championship season. Unfortunately it came in frustrating fashion. Kansas had a 14–7 lead as the time ran down. Penn State took the ball after a punt with a little more than a minute left. Quarterback Chuck Burkhart threw a long pass to Bob Campbell that brought the Nittany Lions to the Kansas 3-yard line.

The next play went for no gain. The one after that did, too. Then on third down, Burkhart kept the ball and ran around the left end for a touchdown. There was no overtime then, so an extra point would have virtually guaranteed a tie. Instead, Paterno called for a two-point conversion. Burkhart's pass was knocked down, and Penn State was about to come up short.

But wait. There was a flag on the field. The officials spotted 12 men on the Kansas defense, a penalty that required a redo. Campbell carried the ball into the end zone on the second try, pushing the Nittany Lions to a 15–14 win.

The story turned stranger still. The Jayhawks actually had an extra player on the field for that whole series of plays. The officials just did not notice right away. As the disappointed Kansas coaches and players later explained, there was confusion after Penn State completed the long pass to Campbell. The Jayhawks

Kansas coach Pepper Rodgers, *left*, and Penn State coach Joe Paterno, *right*, stand with Kansas governor Robert Docking at a luncheon held before the 1969 Orange Bowl.

were supposed to switch to their goal-line defense. When two substitutes came in, only one player went out. It stayed that way for the next several plays.

The other man who was supposed to go to the sideline was Rick Abernathy, a senior linebacker. He was so devastated that he cried afterward in the locker room.

"I was crushed. I have never had a more hollow feeling in my life," Abernathy said. "I wanted to melt into the grass."

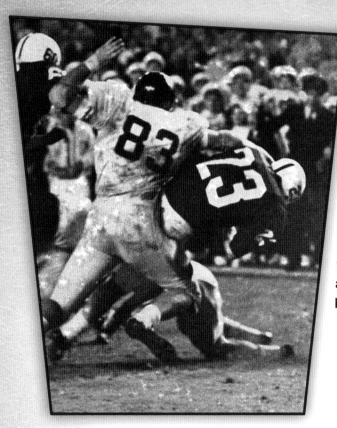

Penn State halfback Bob Campbell, *right*, dives into the end zone for the game-winning two-point conversion against Kansas in the 1969 Orange Bowl.

Football is filled with turning points, though, and Kansas was kicking itself about other missed opportunities. The Jayhawks had a fourth-and-1 from the Penn State 5-yard line earlier in the fourth quarter. They gave the ball to John Riggins, their rugged running back known as "The Diesel." Riggins went on to a long NFL career with the New York Jets and Washington Redskins.

But The Diesel got stopped for no gain on this run. The Jayhawks were left to wonder what would have happened if they tried a field goal instead. A successful kick there would have given Kansas a 17–7 lead, perhaps enough of a cushion to keep Penn State from coming back.

Penn State returned to Miami after the 1969 season and beat Missouri for back-to-back Orange Bowl victories. Despite finishing undefeated both times, the Nittany Lions were not voted national champions either of those years. Paterno pointed to the Orange Bowl appearances, though, for helping establish the program as a national power. Finally the Nittany Lions could recruit the best players in the Rust Belt states against Michigan, Notre Dame, and Ohio State.

HALFTIME MEETS BIG-TIME

Orange Bowl founder Earnie Seiler became known as the "Mad Genius." One clear sign of his creative energy was with the halftime show. The first game in 1935 featured the Miami Hurricanes band parading around the field and students throwing oranges to the spectators. Shows became more elaborate as the years went on. In 1983, the theme was games. One float featured a giant Rubik's Cube measuring 15 feet (4.6 m) high and 35 feet (10.7 m) wide with colored lighting behind 80 squares. To this day, the Orange Bowl halftime show remains a favorite of fans around the country.

"In 1969, there was a lot of comment that it was a one-time thing," Paterno said. "They kept saying it wouldn't last." Four hundred-plus victories later, apparently "they" were wrong.

Raghib "Rocket" Ismail, shown returning a kickoff for a touchdown in a 1990 game against Miami, was one of the fastest players in Notre Dame history.

1991 GROUNDING THE ROCKET

Colorado vs. Notre Dame

They called him "Rocket."

Raghib Ismail was his name, and he was fast. Some consider him to be the speediest player in Notre Dame history. He reportedly ran a 40-yard dash for NFL scouts in a lightning-quick 4.28 seconds. He played wide receiver and running back, and he was a kick returner, too. His presence on the field from 1988 to 1990 gave the Fighting Irish quite an advantage.

Notre Dame won the national championship in Ismail's freshman season and was a strong contender again the next year. The Irish lost in the 1989 regular season to Miami, though, ending their 23-game winning streak. The Hurricanes took the title that year instead.

Notre Dame still finished strong in the Orange Bowl with a 21-6 win against Colorado. Ismail scored on a 35-yard reverse in the game, another example of his versatile talent.

Notre Dame remained one of the top teams in the country in 1990. Behind coach Bill McCartney, Colorado stayed strong, too. Interrupting the control Nebraska or Oklahoma usually had on the Big 8, the Buffaloes again qualified for the Orange Bowl. They had tied Tennessee and lost by one point to Illinois during a difficult nonconference schedule. They beat Stanford, Texas, and Washington, though. Then they cruised through the Big 8 undefeated, destined again for Miami.

Ismail was not the only NFL prospect who played for the Irish, of course. When he skipped his senior season to turn pro, Ismail was one of 10 Notre Dame players chosen in the 1991 NFL Draft. So when the Buffs took their number-one national ranking into the Orange Bowl that night, the fifth-ranked Irish were not intimidated. But they had their hands full.

They did not make it easy on themselves, either. Notre Dame committed five turnovers in the rematch. The Irish had an extra point blocked in the second quarter, too. That play came back to bite them later.

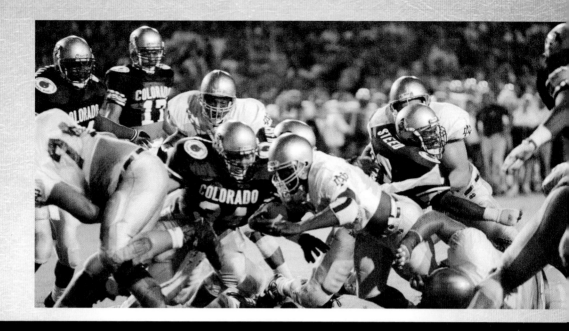

Notre Dame running back Ricky Watters, *center*, scores a touchdown in the second quarter of the 1991 Orange Bowl.

Colorado had trouble moving the ball against Notre Dame's stiff defense. The Buffaloes still trailed 9–3 in the third quarter, with starting quarterback Darian Hagan lost to a knee injury. But backup Charles Johnson gave the Buffs a boost. The Irish had trouble adjusting to a different style with Johnson under center. Colorado's offense began to chip away at the Notre Dame defense.

Meanwhile, Irish running backs Tony Brooks and Ricky Watters fumbled on consecutive third-quarter possessions, giving Colorado a spark. Tailback Eric Bieniemy scored to put the Buffs ahead 10–9. Johnson completed all three of his passes on that drive to get the Buffs close to the goal line.

Notre Dame's Raghib Ismail is smothered by teammates after Ismail returned a punt 91 yards for the apparent go-ahead touchdown late in the 1991 Orange Bowl. The play was called back because of a penalty, and Colorado went on to win 10–9.

But the Irish had one more chance. Colorado was forced to punt with 43 seconds left in the game. Ismail waited to return it. He caught the ball, weaved his way through the coverage, and raced into the end zone for what appeared to be a 91-yard touchdown.

However, Notre Dame was called for a clipping penalty. The score did not count. Five plays later, quarterback Rick Mirer threw the last of his three interceptions. For the first time, Colorado became national champions.

The Buffaloes had a lot to play for that year. There was the matter of revenge against the Irish after losing to them in the previous Orange Bowl. But many of the older players also carried a special inspiration. His name was Sal Aunese, and he died of stomach cancer on September 23, 1989, at age 21.

Aunese had joined the team in 1987 after sitting out his freshman season to focus on school. He was a tough, option-style quarterback from San Diego, one of the first big-time recruits McCartney landed there.

Aunese ran the wishbone offense like a whiz, but at the end of his junior year he began to feel sick. He played poorly in Colorado's bowl game. By the time he was diagnosed with the disease the next spring, Aunese was given six months to live.

The Buffaloes dedicated that 1989 season to him. In 1990, his spirit was still strong around the program. After that dramatic one-point win in the Orange Bowl, McCartney brought home a specially made No. 8 jersey to give to Aunese's son.

HURRICANES AT HOME

Miami became one of the best programs in the country in the 1980s. The Hurricanes won four national championships between the 1983 and 1991 seasons. Three of those were capped by a victory in the Orange Bowl on their home turf. In the 1992 game, they dominated Nebraska. The Huskers had the most productive offense in the country that year, but they lost 22–0. That was the first time in 221 games they failed to score.

Nebraska's Ahman Green lands on his head after being tackled by the Tennessee defense during the 1998 Orange Bowl.

5

1998
OSBORNE OUT
Nebraska vs. Tennessee

Bob Devaney built the Nebraska program into a powerhouse during the 1960s and early 1970s. His successor, Tom Osborne, kept it running strong. Osborne's 25-year career in charge of the Huskers came to an end in the 1997 season. The Orange Bowl provided a fitting conclusion to his dominant run.

The Huskers racked up 534 yards of offense in a 42–17 win against Tennessee. They rushed for an eye-popping 409 yards. Osborne, humble to the end, did not want to take any of the glory from his players.

"They're the guys who did it. I just stood there," Osborne said after his 255th and final victory.

Ahman Green rushed for 206 yards, an Orange Bowl record that earned him the game's Most Valuable Player

(MVP) award. He left school early for the NFL draft soon after the game. Green finished that season with 2,083 rushing yards, averaging 6.7 yards every time he ran the ball.

Tennessee's quarterback was future NFL legend Peyton Manning, who had decided to return for his senior year. He hoped to win the Heisman Trophy and the national championship, both goals that he narrowly missed. But Manning further established himself as a legend in Tennessee. They named animals at the zoo in Knoxville, Tennessee, after him. And there were soon a lot of babies in Tennessee named Peyton.

Manning did not play his best on the night of his last college game. He completed 21 of 31 passes, but for only 134 yards. He threw for one touchdown and had one pass intercepted. Any chance the Volunteers had was wiped out in the first half when they turned the ball over on three straight possessions.

THE FAMOUS FUMBLEROOSKI

The 1984 Orange Bowl was best remembered for the failed two-point conversion by Nebraska with 48 seconds left. The play gave Miami a 31–30 victory and the national title. Earlier that night there was an even more unique play. It was a hidden-ball trick, known as a "Fumblerooski." Huskers quarterback Turner Gill dropped the snap on purpose before running right, pretending he had the ball. Right guard Dean Steinkuhler scooped up the "fumble" and ran around the left end for a 19-yard touchdown.

Nebraska quarterback Scott Frost helped the Huskers control the 1998 Orange Bowl with his running. He only completed nine passes, but he ran for three touchdowns in Nebraska's victory.

Nebraska's pass rush forced Manning to hurry a lot of his throws. He was playing on a sore right knee that had bothered him that year. It was infected badly enough to send him to the hospital for a few days for treatment before the game.

"I love Peyton Manning. He's almost like a son in a lot of ways that you see go on," coach Phil Fulmer said. "In this game you have to say good-bye. You can't pay them to stay another year. If I could figure out how to do that, I would."

Nebraska quarterback Scott Frost did not throw much in the Huskers' option offense. He came through

Tennessee quarterback Peyton Manning grimaces as his Tennessee Volunteers lose to Nebraska 42–17 in the 1998 Orange Bowl.

when he needed to, though. He connected on 9 of 12 passes for 125 yards. More important, he ran for three touchdowns.

The 1998 season was one of the many that prompted changes to the postseason setup. Without a tournament to determine a final winner, the champion was left to a vote. Going into the bowl games, Michigan was ranked number one in the nation. Nebraska was ranked second and Tennessee was third. Michigan beat Washington State in the Rose Bowl the day before the Orange Bowl was played. That made the Nebraska–Tennessee

Nebraska coach Tom Osborne went out on top, ending his 25-year career with a blowout victory over Tennessee in the 1998 Orange Bowl.

matchup meaningless in the minds of some voters. But others obviously disagreed.

Players had to watch TV after the Orange Bowl to find out the poll results. The coaches gave a slight edge to Nebraska for the top spot in their poll, but Michigan was media's choice as the number-one team. It was the third time in four seasons that Osborne and the Huskers had at least a share of the national title.

"We were so loud when we saw it, the hotel security had to come up to tell us to be quiet," Nebraska defensive end Grant Wistrom said.

Clemson wide receiver Sammy Watkins scores a touchdown against West Virginia in the first half of the 2012 Orange Bowl.

6

2012
CATCH US
IF YOU CAN
West Virginia vs. Clemson

Growing up, Geno Smith lived close to the Orange Bowl stadium. He lived so close, in fact, that he could sit outside his house and watch games on the big video screen in the stadium's upper deck.

Smith loved to play football as much as he loved to watch it. The Orange Bowl even helped him play through a grant to a local organization. Years after Smith took part in the Orange Bowl Youth Football Alliance, he took over as the starting quarterback for the West Virginia Mountaineers.

Eventually Smith got a rare opportunity to play in front of his hometown fans. The exciting quarterback led the Mountaineers to the Orange Bowl after the 2011 season. Their opponent was ACC champion Clemson.

Clemson quarterback Tajh Boyd drops back to pass against West Virginia in the 2012 Orange Bowl.

And there was no secret what the theme of this game would be: offense, offense, offense.

The Tigers also had a talented quarterback in Tajh Boyd. They had a freshman wide receiver named Sammy Watkins, who went on to be the fourth pick in the 2014 NFL Draft by the Buffalo Bills. Watkins was one of the few true freshmen to be named a first-team All-American, joining future NFL stars Herschel Walker, Marshall Faulk, and Adrian Peterson from the past.

"Somebody had better check his birth certificate, because there's no way this kid is 18," Tigers teammate Dwayne Allen said that week.

West Virginia quarterback Geno Smith had a happy homecoming with a victory over Clemson in the 2012 Orange Bowl.

Both teams wound up with three losses that year, leaving them out of the national championship picture. But that did not make the game any less entertaining.

Clemson beat Virginia Tech twice and Florida State once to take their first ACC title in 20 years. But the Tigers gave up 30 points or more in six games that year. That made the Tigers vulnerable against Smith and West Virginia's wide-open attack.

Smith set a bunch of Orange Bowl records on that night. The future New York Jets quarterback threw

West Virginia safety
Darwin Cook streaks
down the sideline on a
99-yard fumble return
for a touchdown that
was the key play in the
2012 Orange Bowl.

for six touchdown passes and 401 yards. He ran for a score, too. Fellow future first-round NFL Draft pick Tavon Austin caught four of the touchdown tosses. The Mountaineers racked up 589 yards and won 70–33.

Their 70 points were the most ever by a team in bowl game history. But it could have been an even worse beating. West Virginia had 49 points by halftime, thanks to a five-touchdown second quarter. The Mountaineers scored three touchdowns in the final 2:29 of the quarter. But the West Virginia defense provided the key moment of the game.

Clemson was trailing only 21–17 early in the second quarter. The Tigers were driving, and it appeared they were about to take the lead as running back Andre Ellington ran up the middle toward the goal line. But when Ellington hit the pile, the ball popped out. Safety Darwin Cook picked it up and ran 99 yards untouched the other way. That one play resulted in a 14-point swing. West Virginia was ahead 28–17, instead of trailing 24–21.

Boyd had an interception and a fumble on consecutive plays later in that first half. The first major bowl game appearance in 30 years by the Tigers was a rough one. But they were not deterred.

"It won't be 30 years. We'll be back," coach Dabo Swinney said.

Sure enough, Clemson returned to the Orange Bowl two seasons later. The Tigers were victorious that time, 40–35 against Ohio State.

OBIE THE ORANGE

The Orange Bowl has a mascot named Obie. Being an orange can be rough stuff. West Virginia safety Darwin Cook was running through the end zone after returning a fumble for a touchdown during the 2012 game against Clemson. He leaped at the constantly smiling citrus fruit in celebration. His momentum carried them both to the ground. Afterward, Cook found out a woman was wearing the costume. "I did not know you were a girl. I apologize," he told her.

TIMELINE

1935
Bucknell beats Miami 26–0 in the first Orange Bowl at Miami Field.

1936
CBS conducts the first nationwide radio broadcast of game.

1938
A new stadium opens with the lowest Orange Bowl score ever: Auburn 6, Michigan State 0.

1953
CBS televises the Orange Bowl nationally for the first time.

1963
President John F. Kennedy watches Alabama beat Oklahoma 17–0.

1965
Texas beats Alabama 21–17 in the first Orange Bowl played at night.

1972
Nebraska wins its second straight national championship after beating Alabama 38–6.

1973
Nebraska becomes the first team to appear in three straight Orange Bowls.

1976
Oklahoma wins the national title at the Orange Bowl for the second time, beating Michigan 14–6.

1982
Clemson beats Nebraska 22–15 to win its first national championship.

1984
Miami beats Nebraska 31–30 to win its first national championship.

1995
Nebraska wins the national title with its first Orange Bowl win in four tries against Miami.

1996
The Orange Bowl is played on New Year's Eve and in the Miami Dolphins' stadium for the first time.

1999
The game returns to Orange Bowl stadium one last time.

2000
Michigan beats Alabama 35–34 in the first overtime Orange Bowl.

2006
Penn State needs triple overtime to beat Florida State 26–23 in the longest Orange Bowl ever.

2012
West Virginia beats Clemson 70–33 in the highest-scoring Orange Bowl in history.

BOWL RECORDS

Most rushing yards
206, Ahman Green, Nebraska vs. Tennessee, 1998

Longest run from scrimmage
94 yards, Larry Smith, Florida vs. Georgia Tech, 1967

Most passing yards
453, Dak Prescott, Mississippi State vs. Georgia Tech, December 2014

Most touchdown passes
6, Geno Smith, West Virginia vs. Clemson, 2012

Longest touchdown reception
79 yards, Ross Coyle, Oklahoma vs. Syracuse, 1959

Most receiving yards
227, Sammy Watkins, Clemson vs. Ohio State, January 2014

Most sacks
4, Rusty Medearis, Miami vs. Nebraska, 1992

Most tackles
31, Lee Roy Jordan, Alabama vs. Oklahoma, 1963

Most wins
12, Oklahoma

Most losses
9, Nebraska

Widest margin of victory
55 points, Alabama (61) vs. Syracuse (6), 1953

*through the December 2014 Orange Bowl

QUOTES AND ANECDOTES

"I coached the only Kansas team ever to win the Big 8 championship, and I have spent the rest of my life explaining that we lost the Orange Bowl with 12 men on the field." — Kansas coach Pepper Rodgers, reflecting on the 15–14 loss to Penn State in 1969

"I was disappointed that someone from our league did not step up and say, 'This isn't right.' We've got enough trouble in our conference knocking each other off without knocking each other off in a bowl." — Nebraska coach Tom Osborne, disappointed in having to play Oklahoma for a second time that season in the 1979 Orange Bowl

"We are still in the selling business at Florida State. We are a young school and not in a conference." — Florida State coach Bobby Bowden, on his decision to wear a microphone for the telecast of the 1980 Orange Bowl against Oklahoma

Tom Brady won a Super Bowl with the New England Patriots in his second NFL season, but two years prior to that he finished his college career at Michigan with an Orange Bowl victory. Brady still has the Orange Bowl record with 34 pass completions in that 35–34 overtime win against Alabama. He threw 46 times, with four touchdowns.

"It was like a virus." — Clemson coach Dabo Swinney, after West Virginia overwhelmed his team with a 70–33 win in the 2012 Orange Bowl, fueled by a 35-point second quarter

GLOSSARY

conference

A group of schools that join together to create a league for their sports teams. The Big 12 Conference and Atlantic Coast Conference are examples.

fumble

When a player with the ball loses possession, allowing the defense the opportunity to recover it.

goal line

The edge of the end zone that a player must cross with the ball to score a touchdown.

interception

When a defensive player catches a pass instead of the offensive player.

option

A style of offense or a particular play in which the quarterback can either hand the ball off, carry it himself, pitch it back to another player, or drop back to pass.

reverse

A play in which the offensive line blocks one way and a receiver takes a handoff from the quarterback and runs around the opposite end.

snap

The start of each play begins when the center hikes the ball between his legs to a player behind him, usually the quarterback.

two-point conversion

An option for teams that have scored a touchdown to try a running or passing play from the 3-yard line for two points, instead of kicking for one point.

wishbone

A style of offense that features a quarterback, a fullback, and two halfbacks, all of whom are threats to run the ball.

FOR MORE INFORMATION

Further Reading

Howell, Brian. *Miami Hurricanes*. Minneapolis, MN: Abdo Publishing, 2013.

Monnig, Alex. *Nebraska Cornhuskers*. Minneapolis, MN: Abdo Publishing, 2013.

Monnig, Alex. *Oklahoma Sooners*. Minneapolis, MN: Abdo Publishing, 2013.

Smith, Loran. *Fifty Years on the Fifty: The Orange Bowl Story*. New York: East Woods, 1983.

Websites

To learn more about Bowl Games of College Football, visit **booklinks.abdopublishing.com**. These links are routinely monitored and updated to provide the most current information available.

Place to Visit

College Football Hall of Fame

250 Marietta Street NW

Atlanta, Georgia 30313

404-880-4800

www.cfbhall.com

This hall of fame and museum highlights the greatest players and moments in the history of college football. Relocated from South Bend, Indiana, in 2014, it includes multiple galleries, a theater, and an interactive area where fans can test their football skills.

INDEX

About the Author

Dave Campbell has been a sports writer for the Associated Press since 2000, reporting on the major Minnesota teams and other national stories for the worldwide wire service. He graduated from the University of St. Thomas in St. Paul, Minnesota, with a degree in print journalism. He lives in Minneapolis with his wife. He was born in Illinois and raised in Wisconsin, where playing football for LaCrosse Central High School was one of his proudest life experiences. His passion for sports started at a young age, with college football always at the top of the list.